Speaking for my Self

Speaking for my Self

Twelve women poets
in their seventies and eighties

Edited by Sondra Zeidenstein

Chicory Blue Press, Inc.

Goshen, Connecticut

Chicory Blue Press, Inc.
Goshen, Connecticut 06756
© 2014 Sondra Zeidenstein. All rights reserved.
Printed in the United States of America.

Book Designer: Virginia Anstett
Cover photograph: Sondra Zeidenstein

www.chicorybluepress.com

Library of Congress Cataloging-in-Publication Data

Speaking for my self : twelve women poets in their seventies and eighties / Sondra Zeidenstein.
    pages cm.
ISBN 978-1-887344-14-2 (pbk.:alk. paper)
1. Older people's writings, American. 2. Older women—Literary collections. 3. American
literature—Women authors. I. Zeidenstein, Sondra, editor of compilation.

PS508.A44S64   2014
810.8'09285—dc23

2013031665

for George

Speaking for my Self   v

vi

Contents

Introduction   xi

Betty Buchsbaum
   Altered State   3
   What Matters   4
   Need   6
   Daphne   7
   The Chills   9

Phoebe Hoss
   O Carapace!   13
   A Splotch of Yellow   14
   Ms Maybe Resists the Sirens' Song   15
   Message to Hamas   16
   As Unexpected as Snow in Jerusalem   17

Nancy Kassell
   Celestial Navigation   21
   We Love Those Best   22
   81 Eddy St. San Francisco, CA   23
   262 Capricorn Ave. Oakland, CA   24
   Grounded   25

Rita Brady Kiefer
   Meteors   29
   Sister Vincent's Lexicon   30
   Holding   31
   Afghan Unraveling   32
   Panning   33

Liane Ellison Norman
   Lately   37
   Knitting Needle   39
   Rules   40
   Inheritance   41
   Flick of a Bird   43

Margaret Randall

Wherever You Are, Lois Lane   47
Every Equation Up For Grabs   48
Clean Red and Black   49
Writing on the Body   50
Wrong and Wrong   51

Myra Shapiro

Lake Damariscotta   59
Gold Star Girl   60
The Bouquet   61
March   63
At the End of the Play   64

Carole Stone

Inky Heart   67
Cigars   68
Rooftop   69
Cross   70
Cold Edge   71

Florence Weinberger

Marrowbones   75
Humming   76
It's Not Chinatown   77
Stephen Hawking's Reasoning   78
My two daughters drop me off at the museum   79

Nellie Wong

When I Am Breathing   83
Wintry Interlude   84
Consumed   86
Woman in Red Shoes   88
I Know My Mother Better All the Time   89

Sondra Zeidenstein

In the Middle of the Night   93
Time Zones   95

Subjection of Women   98
Allan Ginsburg   100
History   102

Geraldine Zetzel
Worldly Goods   107
Lying   109
Carmelina   111
Joy   113
Mt. Fuji Between the Waves Off the Coast of Kanagawa   114

About the Poets   117

Credits   123

x

Introduction

The poets in *Speaking for my Self* are twelve American women still writing and publishing poems in their seventies and eighties. They live in New York, California, New Jersey, Massachusetts, Colorado, Connecticut, Oregon and Pennsylvania. I have followed the work of almost all of them for decades. Seven of these poets have been published singly or in anthologies by Chicory Blue Press in the twenty-five years it has been at work as a feminist literary press focusing on the writing of older women. The others have come to my attention as older women poets more recently.

A year ago I told these writers about my plans for this anthology and asked them to send me a sheaf of recent work, ten or so poems, written after they were seventy-five. I told them I was not looking particularly for poems about aging, just poems written *in* age: what is on our hearts as old women poets looking ahead, back, around. I didn't know what the resulting collection of sixty poems would look like, though I spent a lot of time daydreaming about what might be revealed by such a concentration of old women writers in our mostly silenced generation.

Not that we haven't read the work of old poets increasingly in recent years. More men than women, of course—W.S. Merwin, Galway Kinnell, C.K. Williams, Gerald Stern, for starters. I read each of them ardently for the proven beauty of their work and to learn something I don't yet know about the long-lived life. Among old women, I have turned in the last decade to Maxine Kumin, to Marie Ponsot, to the late Lucille Clifton, the late Grace Paley, the late Adrienne Rich and Ruth Stone. I have so wished there were more old women poets who were well published.

For this volume, I have sought out those of my cohorts, born in the twenties and thirties, who had the chance to take up writing, often later in life, and didn't die young, those who had the talent and support and courage to devote time to a pursuit that was not likely to pay off. Each poet in this volume is a "self," an individual, an accomplished poet. Each has a distinct voice. All identify as poets and have had a lot of their work published. Each has willed her life into words. I chose five poems of each poet that captured something important about the poet's individual voice and many-layered sensibility, as well as the commonality of experience among women who came up through the twenties, thirties, forties of the last century into the present.

I chose these poems for the authenticity of voice each poet has found within her generation, for her courage to look life in the face, for her emotion, passion, conviction, for as much nakedness as she dares. (*But* life *is personal*, said Robert Lowell to a poet friend who was worried about his poems being too personal).

Speaking for my Self xi

I chose them for directness and clarity—because there is urgency in our communication. That is what I look for in my life, at my age, writing that "brings news from the inmost being, that deepest level of being which is harder to reach than the underside of the earth's crust, harder to reach than the stratosphere, because it is more safely guarded: by each one of us." *

I am disappointed that there is not more cultural diversity among these writers, although that has always been a sought after goal in what Chicory Blue Press publishes. I hope there will be much more such diversity among older women poets as the next generations and communities of women writers come to age in an atmosphere of less sexism, less racism, less poverty, more access to education, more mentors. In the meantime, I am determined to give a slice of the very silenced generation I belong to another chance to be heard. This has been a mission of mine since I established Chicory Blue Press in the flush of the feminist movement. In the introduction to my website *www.chicoryblue press.com* written quite a few years ago, I put it this way:

"I publish older women writers because I need company. I have always believed that how we imagine our lives, how we make meaning of living, comes largely from literature. The older I get the more I find myself seeking older women writers to tell me about myself. I am still acutely aware of how skewed my understanding of myself was in the years of growing up, entering womanhood, married life, motherhood, when there were not many writers in whose work the texture of my life, my feelings, my side of the story as a woman had been transformed by the imagination. At this stage of my journey through life, I feel alone, again in a largely unimagined world. I need to read what is written from the perspective of older women so I can imagine myself part of a varied, vital community, not as an anonymous, marginalized, stereotyped "senior." But there are not enough of us. From the point of view of age and gender, we are the most underrepresented among published writers; older women writers from minority cultures are even scarcer. I publish older women writers because we are in short supply."

❀ ❀ ❀

When I look over these poems, all sixty of them, as I have again and again, always thrilled and proud that they are coming to my hands, into my care, I find themes or categories in common. We write of loss, justice, compassion, connectedness, love, art, creativity.

*in *The Quest for Christa T.* by Christa Wolf, 1979.

Many of these poems are memories, re-remembered through layers of age, experienced now as more pivotal in shaping our lives, than they once were. In "Splotch of Yellow," **Phoebe Hoss** begins:

> *It's not that some things*
> *are best forgotten; it's that*
> *they can't be…*

Some are about parents and childhood like "I Know My Mother Better All the Time" by **Nellie Wong** or like "Knitting Needle" by **Liane Ellison Norman** in which she writes about her grandmother:

> *She mended, darned,*
> *crocheted a lacy shawl for me, braided a thick wool rug*
> *from our outgrown winter coats. Said she'd performed*
> *abortions on herself with a knitting needle. No details.*

Some are about youthful imaginings of self:

> *I loved to puff a cigarillo in the West Village*
> *like "Vincent" Millay. Inhaling desire*

by **Carole Stone.**

Or shared history, as I write in "History":

> *I was twenty-five, in Brooklyn, with two toddlers,*
> *when I watched nine black children in their Sunday best*
> *stopped by the Little Rock National Guard.*

Some of the poems are about writing poems: Again, **Phoebe Hoss**, in "Ms Maybe Resists The Sirens' Song":

> *Age presses on her, the shadow of*
> *unimaginable finality creeping*
> *ever closer. Ever farther off*
> *the poems she's ever longed to write.*

In "The Bouquet," **Myra Shapiro** revives her earliest memory of poetry:

> *Nature frightened me-*
> *you could die from it-*
> *so I would stay in bed*
> *with A Child's Garden*

Speaking for my Self xiii

of Verses, *rescued*
from the heaving
and holding breaths
of asthma.

Many of the poems are inspired by art and artists. **Geraldine Zetzel**'s poem "Carmelina" is subheaded, "after Matisse":

What is there to stare at?
remarks your gaze.
No odalisque or nymph,
you wear your nakedness
like a robe of clear water.

Betty Buchsbaum's "Daphne" starts:

The way Bernini felt me up and down
breathing hot on my neck and breast as he turned
my head to look back, terrified, Apollo
at my heels.

Myra Shapiro refers to recent art in "At the End of the Play":

"Make yourself an angel,"
the Victorian doctor's wife asks of him
in a new play. In the Next Room.

"Open your arms," and, like a child,
he does. In the snow he disrobes
for her. For all of us.

Florence Weinberger, in her poem, "My two daughters drop me off at the museum," depends on the deep comfort of art:

I am so lucky having
good weather and this is what I wanted to be celebrated on my
eightieth birthday with my two daughters no husbands no children
just us and I got to see this astonishing painting

Some of the most moving poems, naturally, are about the many stages of love: love and relationship, the decades long love that has been or will be severed, the anticipation of loss. **Nancy Kassell**'s compact poem "We Love Those Best" begins:

xiv

We love those best whom we need the most.

In "Panning," **Rita Brady Kiefer** hopes:

Morning on predictable fall morning
intimations of fading
but at the end some green luck
might make us vanish together

My poem, "In The Middle of the Night," begins:

Now that we've stopped 'making love'
because my old bones hurt so…

Many are about death but none as blunt as **Liane Ellison Norman**'s "Lately" which begins:

I've been rehearsing
death- the next big thing:
like choosing and blooming at
the right college; like finding
the only man I've loved
and lived with
more than half a century

Or as piercingly expressed as **Nancy Kassell**'s "Celestial Navigation":

I know your point of departure,
I know how much time has elapsed.
What I don't know is your course and speed,
how to make reckoning
for the dead.

Some are unexpected, like **Betty Buchsbaum**'s conclusion to "Need:"

As for me at eighty, after a long,
lucky run, many full seasons,
is it before my time
to want, some days,
to be less needed?

There are many poems of compassion, both for those close by, including our selves, and, more often, a reaching out and drawing in of those who are suffering all over the world. It was so wonderful for me to find these poets in

Speaking for my Self xv

Speaking for my Self calling out over and over a passion for justice. They imagine, embrace, draw to their poetry bosoms, fiercely, lovingly, those who are wronged. As in **Margaret Randall**'s catalogue of a poem "Wrong and Wrong" which ends with:

> *Tenderness is not collateral damage,*
> *partial lines scrawled across a page*
> *found among the ruins*
> *of all our lives.*

As in **Rita Brady Kiefer**'s heart nourishing poem "Meteors" to Malala, the Pakistani girl who was shot for seeking to learn:

> *Did your eyes flash terror when they hijacked your school bus,*
> *one of the men snarling your name down the aisle,*
> *scanning each innocent face before lighting on yours?*

As in **Nellie Wong**'s poem, "Consumed," for the

> *temporary worker*
> *stampeded to death at 5:00 A.M.*
> *by 200 shoppers.*

And in **Margaret Randall**'s "Every Equation Up For Grabs,"

> *when nature on nature*
> *gives way to human interference,*
> *man against nature and man against man*
> *every assumption stumbles,*
> *every equation is up for grabs.*

There is humor in these poems. There is joy. In a way, all the poems are about joy, the sensory details affirmations of the natural world, of the body, as in **Geraldine Zetzel**'s poem, "Joy":

> *A wet leaf glints in the sun*
> *a jay calls out in the woods*
> *Coolness touches my face*
> *for a moment: this edge of joy…*

There is little, if anything, about the consolation of religion which takes a back seat for this generation of writers. **Carole Stone** starts her poem "Cross":

> *God could have gotten Jesus down*

from the Cross,
blood staining his side
his gaunt body stretched out.
The same Old Testament deity
who didn't save the Jews.

Florence Weinberger reaches for solace in unconventional ways in her poem "Humming":

> *To those who have brought my humming to my attention, who understand that sometimes my hum is a whistle in the dark and sometimes it is grieving, I give thanks.*

We are, as Allan Ginsburg kept reminding us, all in this together.

❈   ❈   ❈

The first book Chicory Blue Press published more than twenty-five years ago is *A Wider Giving: Women Writing after a Long Silence.* This book celebrated women of my generation who started writing "seriously" after the age of forty-five. It owed its existence partly to Tillie Olsen's ground breaking book, *Silences,* in which Olsen examines the various ways in which writers who had begun to create were silenced: for example, by poverty, by exclusion, by the necessity for political action, by censorship, by lack of time and support, by alcoholism and suicide. Women were silenced by all these obstacles, but especially by what we have come to call sexism.

Because such oppression is often internalized and experienced as inadequacy, it is often hard to identify and combat. In breaking the silence imposed by their culture, women have had to give themselves time and permission, seek out training, face rejection and self-doubt, fight the negativity sometimes ingested from their own mothers, begin to develop their craft and, hardest of all, summon the strength again and again to continue. It is no wonder that Adrienne Rich said once, in a talk about Ann Sexton, *any woman who writes is a survivor.*

❈   ❈   ❈

The writers I published in *A Wider Giving* were all women who started late or returned to writing late. Several of the writers in this book, *Speaking for my Self,* are of this sort. Others have been writing all their lives. All of them have achieved recognition. All of them have continued into age. They've come through every obstacle that oppresses women, and now old women, to shut them up.

Speaking for my Self   xvii

A number of poets I've published in my press's twenty-five year life are gone. Carrie McCray from South Carolina, the granddaughter of a slave, turned to poetry, which I published, in her seventies. She died in her nineties. But what happened to the Louisiana poet who had a leaning toward concrete poetry and folk tales, full of energy and toughness and humor? She was not encouraged. Quite a few of the poets I've published over the last couple of decades have stopped writing. Or been stopped by death. There is much loss.

But many have kept on. We are not alone, though our voices travel these long years through a world that hasn't had much patience for us speaking for our selves. (Why do I think of the raped women in the armed forces looking at the stony faces and beribboned chests of the chain of command who for the most part don't think sexual assault is anything to make such a big fuss about).

And now this book, *Speaking for my Self*, which is a concentrate of age. In it, we move in the company of old women writers who are braving age, twelve poets giving shape to their/our lives, warming and reassuring us that we are alive and even mouthy. I am so grateful for what writing has given us, a sense of self, a commitment to speak from it, against conventional culture, forces that would silence us all.

What a wasteland would lie ahead of us if we were not humanizing existence to the edge of incapacity and death, bringing that experience into the fold. Why should I feel isolated, as if I am out here alone, when there are these eleven other women (and how many more!) I am journeying with, scarves around our foreheads, canteens over our shoulders, sturdy hiking sticks, stout ones, in our fists as we plough on, speaking for our selves. It's a long, hard slog, but if it feels sometimes like sorrow, more often it feels like joy.

Betty Buchsbaum

Altered State

*"The Gates" Central Park, March, 2005.
Installation by Christo and Jean Claude*

Tramped this park dawn to dusk for two days
wanting to know it
in its short-lived altered state.
Though alone, I was never lonely
my body a tireless companion
a young, excited guide with no taste
for standing still to mull *what is it? do I get it?*
It walked me miles of winding paths
through gates of pleated saffron
flowing from tall frames
gates that didn't divide, shut out
but marked a procession of bright thresholds
step by wintry step I moved
through opening after opening
the orange-yellow of saffron
a weave of hot sun, golden moon
marooned at times in stillness
or billowing like sails
or shimmering on pond and lake
like paint on a watery canvas
and always highlighting
the varied slant and width of footpaths
frames molded to curves
distinct as those of the human body
and when I doubled back
crossing north to south or east to west
never the same light never the same bare branches
etched in folds of saffron
and rarely the same cold or warm wet or dry
and no ultimate peak or summit
simply no end to my desire to walk winding paths
of unguarded joyous openings—

oh body, just remember!

Betty Buchsbaum 3

What Matters

when spirit falters
grey and listless in one's aging body?

This small, hidden refuge in your garden
where you write this morning

you cloistered on all sides
by lilies, roses, honeysuckle, lavender?

And the path that led you here?—
not just the bluestone pavers

leading from the kitchen door
but the circling years of your long marriage

and the children and their children
who come here Sundays?

And your desire, after daughters
left home, to create this garden.

Then summer, this cloudless,
blue sky, doesn't it matter

after a hard, cold, icy winter
when you and your beloved were afraid to fall?—

these zero-gravity lawn chairs lifting
our legs off the ground as we lie back in the sun,

defying the way our shrinking frames
are being pulled down to earth

like down-going elevators
passing our grandchildren on the way up.

And after his long season of pain
his new right knee, bursitis-free shoulder,

gout-free toe, staph-free body—matter.
Also our voices in this garden: blending,

crossing over and under each other
like two old, familiar hands on the piano;

and our silences, like floating together in slightly
bouncy sea water and not sinking—

the not sinking yet…
today it matters.

Betty Buchsbaum

Need

This morning I'd like the drooping lilies
to right themselves
without me

but they need me to tie their long stems
to tall bamboo rods
so the large, gaudy red and yellow hybrids

won't lean over and hide
the smaller,
freckled pinks,

and so the rainstorm, predicted
for tonight, won't snap their stems or dash
their trumpet-like blooms to earth

before their time
which, for lilies, means not before
several weeks of dazzling show;

as for me at eighty, after a long,
lucky run, many full seasons,
is it *before my time*

to want, some days, to be *less needed?*—
especially not needed
as caretaker, rallying coach, captive ear

to my own tiresome,
fitful mind
and brooding old heart.

Daphne

"Apollo and Daphne," Lorenzo Bernini (Carrara marble)
Villa Borghese, Rome

The way Bernini felt me up and down
breathing hot on my neck and breast as he turned
my head to look back, terrified, Apollo
at my heels. The chase at its climax,
that's what excites god and human.
At least my artist didn't only lust after my body.
He worked hard to chisel his way
into the secret of how I did it, changing
just like that into another form of life.

He never bought my story of a river god father
who heard my cries and fixed it so Apollo,
for all his lunging, grabbed only bark and leaves
of laurel. Poor man! I don't think he had
a father to call out to when being Bernini
got too hard. And I'm no longer angry
that he froze me in transit, still so much a woman
that I'm gawked at from every naked angle.
At first, quite a shock! I was always a loner,

very private, never ran in the woods undressed.
But in five centuries, I've never heard a sly,
dirty word, just *oohs* and *aahs* over the torque
of my fleeing body, my leafy hair, twiggy fingers,
sprouting toes. It's gotten so I *like*
being gazed at, that buzz of admiring talk
going to my head, even feel a little sorry
for all those fingers itching to touch
what guards and ropes forbid. And I like hovering

between worlds: on the verge of what I'm not
quite yet, still not losing all of *me*.
Sometimes I wish I could touch my breast,
thighs—places where flesh meets bark—fingers
feeling for the mystery of *how* one passes over.
My father never told me. And does everyone

Betty Buchsbaum 7

get to do it? Sometimes, glimpsing a tired old face
in the crowd—skin rough—I speculate:
White oak? Silver beech?

The Chills

There she is, my younger self—
a somber-eyed intruder wedged
between my daughter and me
at the kitchen table.
She slipped into the room
on hearing my daughter's
strained voice confide
worrisome news about her child;
bumped her chair legs against mine
when my daughter said, dark eyes
clamped on mine, *I hope, Mom,*
this won't bring on one of your chills.

We both see her clearly, this mom
of her childhood—worried about
a loved one, she'd often draw an afghan
tight around her shoulders
even if the day was hot and humid;
answer in monosyllables,
her voice so flat you'd think
she'd sat on it; stare
at an open book on her lap
her body slumped like a rag doll
as she disappeared,
barely aware she'd vanished.

I reach across my younger self
and hug my beloved daughter,
listen
to what she chooses
to tell me, try to keep
muzzled unruly
questions that might nip
and yap at her nerves.
I do feel chills but refuse
to let them freeze me—only a fool
would squander her old age
by being absent.

Betty Buchsbaum

Phoebe Hoss

O Carapace!

O carapace! O carapace!
Yours is a truly happy face!
Though within it is sleeting and chill and grim,
your smile—your sweet, grave smile—never grows dim.

O carapace! O carapace!
They all love your happy face
who can't see with its eyes or hear with its ears
or feel it burning into their flesh through the years.

O carapace! O carapace!
So perversely happy is your face
I long to rip it off and stick a wild one in its place,
but it's late, too late for any but this happy face.

A Splotch of Yellow

Up here in bed, reading, writing, watching
the slow onset of spring, spying
a single yellow tulip crying by the fence,
the tide in the creek beyond
at the full, its mirror
solid, implacable, I recall
the hours and hours of wailing
night before last, the little boy,
away from home, inconsolable; his patient
parents, their murmuring
voices.
           A scab
tears off memory: a night
forty years ago visiting my parents,
my little boy frantic, his angry
mother slapping, shaking him,
patience far in her future.

It's not that some things
are best forgotten; it's that
they can't be, that a change
of light, a splotch of the yellow
he loved, can spring them from the deep fresh
and untarnished, unsullied, honed
only the sharper by time, by tide.
It's that we must live
with who we've been.

Ms Maybe Resists the Sirens' Song

Age presses on her, the shadow of
unimaginable finality creeping
ever closer. Ever farther off
the poems she's ever longed to write.
So what, she ponders, does she do with her days? Meetings,
friends, doctors—but, first, of course, beckoning
each morning on her doorstep is the folded
Times. She sees herself removing
the elastic, letting the paper pop open,
letting its headlines entrap her
in the news of the day: large issues
and small, war and weddings, market reports
and intriguing films, the purported
rape of a chambermaid, the dastardly
doings on Wall Street, the settled, insidious
opinions of other people—over none of which, she
suddenly realizes, has she one speck of
power. Why, it's an abyss, sucking
her down, a death she can
imagine—and she begins
to claw her way up, pen clenched between her teeth, hoping
she's still got time, resolving to leave the elastic on
until at least lunchtime.

Phoebe Hoss   15

Message to Hamas

Take me.
             I know
how to live as well
as anyone. My blood's
as sweet as anyone's, my flesh
as firm, as vulnerable
to shrapnel, my eyes
as bright, as sharp.
I can pass
in a crowd, my hair
in its braid as thick
as their challah, as glossy
and black as anyone's.
             Take me.
I've brothers, sisters, a father,
a mother who'll praise Allah
for my deed.
             Take me.
A virgin, I carry in my belly
my only power.
             Take me. Take me.
Like anyone, I have grown
up to do this. I am as young
as anyone.
             Take me.

As Unexpected as Snow in Jerusalem

Pedaling indoors this overcast winter
morning, determinedly traveling
nowhere, I glimpse beyond my two high
windows a swathe of cloud heading
slowly southward: an immense gray
feather escaping from the thick
white down of the sky above; a fish
moving, stately in its solitude, through
that high deep; a tongue musing
across my field of vision; a harbinger
of words after drought, of maybe
poetry.

Phoebe Hoss

Nancy Kassell

Celestial Navigation

Item #155. The Smallest Astrolabe in the World. Indo-Persian
c.1630 A.D. Muhammad Muq m's [instrument] is…
mathematically correct and so a proper representation of the
universe in a form small enough to be hidden in a closed hand,
with all the philosophical implications of such an action.

Saul Moskowitz. Catalogue 133

I know your point of departure,
I know how much time has elapsed.
What I don't know is your course and speed,
how to make reckoning
for the dead.

Compass, astrolabe, quadrant,
chronometer, Bowditch's "Practical Navigator"—
none of the tools of historical
technology can locate you. I imagine, though,
you know your way around the universe so well
that someone adjusting a radio telescope or
plotting coordinates in The Global Positioning System
will detect you, a shadow in the interstices of a nebula,
after I am gone.

In the meantime, I have the ephemeris,
the daily shift
in alignment of the planets
of memory, an exquisitely wrought and improper
representation of the universe, which I hold
in the palm of my hand.

Nancy Kassell

We Love Those Best

We love those best whom we need the most.
Beaks open, baby lips nuzzling nipple,
until the heart, against its very form,
four closed chambers, is warmed by need
and opens like a bud, turns full-face flower
to another, letting love exit and
enter, a turn which exposes each
to rapture and uncertainty.

481 Eddy St.
San Francisco, CA

Studio apt. in the Tenderloin, home to
a baby grand I played feverishly to console
myself for a shape-shifting childhood.
I slept on the daybed, Mama in the Murphy,
though never with her lover. With the bed
down, there was no floor space. She worked
late, and I cooked my dinner in the non-
eat-in kitchen (broiled lamb chop, veg, pot).

Walking was one way out. Uphill over Hyde St. to the Bay—
climb and vista an unconscious metaphor for growing up,
though I didn't yet suspect the ambiguities of arrival.
The walk to Union Sq. with its formal plantings, and
the florist Podesta Baldocchi, Maiden Lane, a cul-de-sac
where I breathed the essence of green and bloom and
forgot having to hold my breath against the blast of booze
and stale cigarette smoke from the open door of the bar
downstairs. Farther on, the Mechanics Institute Library,
whose narrow stacks, criss-crossed, cut me loose.

Nancy Kassell   23

262 Capricorn Ave.
Oakland, CA

Scrawny eucalyptus trees, hilltop perch up 67
uneven steps we climbed like mountain goats to
an ether of dream and myth. He would write plays,
I was devoted to scholarship. Even a cat named

Thisbe. Mornings, I set out text, Smyth, Allen &
Greenough, dictionaries on the dining room table.
I read:

> Pre-Socratics parsing the universe
> Thucydides on the war, journal and commentary
> Pindar on talent in the blood
> Aeneas plowing destiny, a new homeland

in between nursing my new baby daughter before
the winter fire. At three o'clock I gave my older girl,
home from school, a snack, and put the books away.

One professor studied my face and intuiting
a certain intensity, prophesied,

You will do lyric.

Dactyls six and five, iamb, choriamb

Later, free

Grounded

> *Maybe it's all thanks to the sun above me. I am always looking up toward the sky.*
>
> Jiroemon Kimura, age 115

He is on good terms with the sky, philosophically speaking
and with wry humor. He doesn't look up to ask to be
someone else or somewhere else, or for something
more. He wants what he has, what anyone
can have who has the grace to notice.

Snow today, or just rain? he wonders as he steps out
to start the day's mail delivery. Pausing at the edge
of the field, he's hoping weather will be good
for the crops he's planted this year—
azuki beans, yams, or rice.

At his birthday celebration he is beaming.
Thank you very much, he says to guests and to the videographer,
showing off the English he recently learned. A squirmy baby,
one of 13 great-great grandchildren, is set in his lap.

Nancy Kassell

Rita Brady Kiefer

Meteors

Did your eyes flash terror when they hijacked your school bus,
one of the men snarling your name down the aisle,
scanning each innocent face before lighting on yours?
What images blazed just before the bullet
grazed your luminous brain, sweet Malala?
At the hospital did you have nightmares: Taliban
instead of your loved olive trees in the orchards
outside your father's classroom, a thousand
points of grief webbing your mother's face.
Or did you dream bright streaks shooting across
a black sky? Not disembodied particles of dust
but flesh and blood women, subversive sisters
from the past? Were their stories familiar?

       A 17th century girl so bent on learning
she hid her body under boys' clothes to go to school.

       A Mexican nun, reproached in an open letter
by a bishop masked with a woman's name,
replied with a learned defense of girls'
and women's *right* to study.

       A female German mystic eleven centuries back
who depicted God as Female.

Why do we doubt the sky is filled with history?
At eleven, Malala, you blogged:
Why aren't girls allowed to learn?
I want to read books. I want to write them.

Incandescent little rebel, you've already begun.

Rita Brady Kiefer

Sister Vincent's Lexicon

In third grade Sister Vincent primed us
for the January feast days
her large white wimple swaying
as the chalk squeaked out big words
like *epiphany* explaining as she wrote
it meant *manifestation* or *revelation*,
"that's no help" I whispered to Mae Thomas,
the Feast of the Circumcision came next
but she wrote nothing beside that.
By the time I'd traced the final "n" we'd moved
on to January 21st and Agnes Virgin-Martyr.
"What's a martyr?" Margaret Holland asked.
"A saint killed for Jesus' sake," Sister said, but
Jackie Barnes's hand shot up. "Why would
God wanna' see someone killed for him?
Why wouldn' God say, 'Put down that sword
an' let Angus go,' S'ter?" but Sallie Toomie
interrupted, "What's a virgin?" then copied
with care Sister Vincent's answer: "The holiest
kind of person." I raised my hand but Sister
called on Dick Mulcahy, the smartest boy.
"That other feast you said before—sir-cum-cishun—
what's that?" but Sister snatched up a pastel picture
of St. Agnes holding a lamb and said we had
no more time for questions, that we should put
our heads down on our desks and pray
ejaculations to our very favorite saint.

Holding
for William Stafford

you no longer leave a shadow on earth,
and for these past twenty years no one
has sighted tracks from your reliable snowshoes.

but then, there's always e-mail:
brief electronic longings sent
into cyberspace, like floating

prayers of a sort, that's how
i'll bring you back, almost like
wording ourselves into flesh as i write.

after all, didn't you promise to hold
whatever tugs the other end?
to hold that string?

Afghan Unraveling

So how do you feel about your buddy's death yesterday?

(camera inconspicuous mic)

Right now I don't really feel

anything at all. I mean I pray for his soul

ya' know. I mean actually I'm kinda' numb, Sir.

I try not to think about it 'cause

when I think about it   sorry   sorry, Sir

when I do, I get this way   so   I'm sorry.

*   OK   yeh…*

Everyone deals, uh, I mean feels it his own way

I try to hide it   'cause ya' know

*   I have to stay one-hundred per cent*

*   sorry.   Ohhh,*

*   I gotta' be an example for*

the other guys   we're soldiers, ya' know.

Panning
(for Jerry)

Even October's eye insinuates:
elk bugling into the wind, aspen shuddering
their yellow response   most mornings
you slip first from bed   your frame tentative
against the muted light while under white down
I am half-drugged from dreams thrumming
under lids what sleep left over

(*such a solid little body shaking his crib*
outside our love room each morning
until one of us yielded
from the beginning he was hard to resist
your mother said of her first-born)

your silhouette now aging but still luring
performs those compelling male rituals: an
intermittent, diminishing splash of water,
hushed jockeys and t-shirt consoling
your skin against clamorous jeans that aim
you down the stairs to an early chill
dissipating as your fingers touch buttons
to bring heat   light   coffee
your headphones poised to catch NPR
and last night's score before the jaunt
down the drive for *The Post*

morning on predictable fall morning
intimations of fading
but at the end some green luck
might make us vanish together
if not and I disappear first
        love
head for some gold stream
sediment pan in hand
                if I am left
I will wander the earth
camera-eye panning
repeating your name

Rita Brady Kiefer   33

Liane Ellison Norman

Lately

I've been rehearsing
death—
the next big thing:

like choosing and blooming at
the right college; like finding
the only man I've loved

and lived with
more than half
a century;

like giving body's
lodgment
to infinitesimal

strangers,
who've blossomed
from blastocysts

to three
particular people.
The daily signs—

too-soon
fatigue,
ache of hoisting

bone and flesh
up stairs,
lacunae

where once the right
word bounded
forward

Liane Ellison Norman   37

like a friendly dog
with a slightly
slimy ball.

Knitting Needle

In memory of my grandmother, Alrena Beatrice Thomas Ellison

A.O. walked out. Alrena and the children lived
in the chicken house, sold eggs and fruit. She baked

Cornish pasties. The children sold them from the wagon
they collected laundry in and took back washed and ironed.

She sold corsets, Avon products door-to-door. At the birth
of each grandchild, put $100 in a bank account, gave us

a set of *Encyclopedia Britannica*. For high school graduation
sent us each a Webster's *Dictionary*. She mended, darned,

crocheted a lacy shawl for me, braided a thick wool rug
from our outgrown winter coats. Said she'd performed

abortions on herself with a knitting needle. No details.
By then she must have known her husband feckless,

but how did she know to guide the long, thin steel up
out of sight inside her blood-drenched folds.

Rules

You can tell a lady by her cuticles,
Mother, the preacher's daughter, said,
and whether she crosses her legs at the ankles.

Her mother, the preacher's wife, decreed
a piano's *legs* were *limbs*, a bull was a *gentleman cow,*
and I should not sew marionette costumes

on the Sabbath. Shoes should never be down
at heel nor seams of stockings crooked. Never
wear blue with green nor red with pink.

No plaid with stripes nor silver with gold.
White shoes between Easter and Labor Day,
neither before nor after. Above all, *never, never,
never let a boy know how smart you are.*

Inheritance

I'd like to drink a cup of coffee with my father
     at the kitchen table, red oak like satin under elbows,

cream colored mugs with wide blue bands, daffodils
     in the blue speckled jug, watching the backyard unwind

to green, trilliums blooming briefly while ferns push up
     their coiled fiddleheads and violets raise small faces.

We'd watch birds at the feeder and the squirrels that soar
     like arias in the ancient, damaged maple.

~

He wrote in his Montana journal, 1936, *to my astonishment*
     I found in the limestone a mass of sea shells! Seashells

4,000 ft. above Vigilante, itself 6,000 ft. above the sea....
     what visionary mollusk ever dreamed that he would be lifted so high!

~

We'd laugh about the coffee sheepherders used to serve us
     from their wagons, along with mutton, sourdough biscuits,

tales of bears, coyotes, derring-do, coffee boiled, re-boiled, more grounds
     added 'til a spoon could stand alone.

~

I want to tell him all that's happened since that half a century ago
     on John Paul Jones Ridge, where he and three friends equipped

with packs, first-aid supplies and tools rode the ski lift to the top,
     hiked, strips of moleskin strapped underside their skis,

the nap for traction, ate lunch, conversed among the trees.
     He led off, a downhill run, when the avalanche—silent

to one companion, a roar to the other—swept him down,
     buried him in fifteen feet of snow.

Liane Ellison Norman

But if by magic we could share that cup of coffee, who would we be?
        He was six months shy of fifty when he died. I'm seventy-three.

~

He was slender, neat, his black brush cut, thick eyebrows,
        clear blue eyes looking out across mountains,

grieving irretrievable loss of soil, fingers showing me stamen
        and anther of a flower.

He read to us in the kitchen as we four did dinner dishes to keep us
        from fighting—Stevenson's *Black Arrow,*

the mysterious eye spying, from tapestry, up to no good,
        Lamb's *Essay on Roast Pig,* his delight in words.

He wrote his young wife, my mother, *Our language is a rich, beautiful one;*
        I love it, and do not like to see it mistreated.

Flick of a Bird

At the end of a marble hall in a sumptuous
art nouveau building—million dollar WPA project—

was my high school writing teacher's classroom.
Even the floors were marble. All Ogden used

the gilded auditorium: Utah Symphony, opera
where Don Jose had to stand on a box to stab

his willowy, doomed Carmen, *Rigoletto's* Gilda
scaling vocal heights long after being stabbed

right where I was sure her lungs must be,
Paul Robeson's full-throated pain and glory.

When my daughter died I came to poetry again.
What delights me are the tiny poems—flick of a bird

quick across my retina—no plot, no argument.
Simply the moment, momentary, momentous.

Liane Ellison Norman

Margaret Randall

Wherever You Are, Lois Lane

Barbie, unwrapped this holiday season
by another million little girls,
ratio of waist to hips
defying anatomy around the world.
Consort Ken still tries to pass
and Clark-slash-Superman
flexes his muscles in the wings.

We rage on behalf of our sisters
behind the burqas, hijabs, veils,
who cannot vote or drive,
are saddened by those Utah wives
with hair rolled back
and skirts about their ankles.

Wherever you are, Lois Lane,
come out of hiding.
We need to talk.

Every Equation Up for Grabs

Mesas stretch their purple fingers across sands
that offer withered *cholla* arms
in tentative embrace.

The monsoons are late this year and cactus aches
to plump green flesh with sustenance.
Dull blooms pale the exuberance

of wetter years. *Piñon* and sage sit staunch.
Yet the snow pack is high and deep
and as it melts

rivers rise above their banks.
Furious currents carve new *arroyos,*
rain arrives to save the *chile* crop.

North and east: sandbags cannot keep the water
from nuclear reactors.
One fear dominoes another.

A butterfly in North America gives birth
to a typhoon in Japan
but when nature on nature

gives way to human interference,
man against nature and man against man
every assumption stumbles,

every equation is up for grabs.

Clean Red and Black

I had to look somewhere so fixed my eyes
on the mother's blue satin blouse,
one side of its collar pulled to the side
baring the starkness of breastbone and loss.

Strands of damp hair repeated their fall
across lips silenced by bullets
made somewhere else.
The small room's heat
lungs under siege.

Walls receded, then pressed against me.
Slowly, with purpose,
I brought my gaze to her son's face:
jaw wrapped in strips of gauze,
clean red and black around his neck.

As in so many grieving homes
before and since
I touched the mother's shoulder
raised my camera, got my shot.

We must tell the world, they insisted,
when I complained I can't
keep doing this. Can't. Won't.
The mothers wept and in my dreams
I fled the disappearing faces of my own children.

Sad body-shaped boxes follow me now:
endless parade of containers,
planks, and shrouds on Palestinian shoulders
or thronging the streets of Soweto, Morazán,
Aleppo, Juárez, Chicago.

We've told the world.
When will the world listen?

Margaret Randall 49

Writing On the Body

At Auschwitz seventy years ago
Yosef Diamant's Nazi captors
tattooed his forearm 157622.
Weapon of erasure
deathblow to identity.

Some survivors hide their numbers
beneath long sleeves
revealing them only to lovers
averting their own eyes.
Others play them on the lottery.

All these years later, the fading digits
whisper horror, reduction, shame.
Writing on the body isn't always demolition.
It can be flag, eagle, naked woman
or indelible signature of love.

Initials, gang signs, drunken whim
or precious anniversary
also shout fidelity, control.
But whose fidelity?
Whose control?

Body writing: the torturer's hand
or memory's balm:
One badge of honor. One hideous scar.
Who writes
and who is written upon.

Today in a city where she hopes
terror can be kept at bay
Yosef's granddaughter Eli
shows him his numbers on her young flesh.
He bends to kiss the bridge of memory.

Wrong and Wrong

1

I boarded my first war train in 1942
when Dad sat one night at the edge of my bed,
faint scent of Old Spice and Army serge:
war as absence,
small tree of loneliness.

Too old for the draft and father of two
the Jew who spun his surname
in jump step with Mother's denial
but hated injustice,
heard the rumors, went to do his part,
fascism chewing at his Scarsdale collar.

For my generation this was The War
That Would End All Wars,
the good war no one challenged,
at least no one on that trusting terrain
where I waged my anxious childhood battles.

Grandpa's honeyed hands pulled me
into his *this is our little secret* war,
his *don't tell or I'll kill you* war,
the dreamy smile his deceptive weapon.

All these years later Dad's garrison cap
remains in my six-year-old hand
though I know he took it with him
to basic training at Fort Knox
and brought it with him on every furlough home.

From awkward accommodation
among recruits
better suited for the battlefield
through honorable discharge
and Tarrytown assembly line

Margaret Randall 51

where he came home from work one day
his arm a web of burnt flesh
hot metal against obstinate desire
resignation rising.

That war was Roger, my dog
they trained to kill
so couldn't send him back to a child
the official letter said.

Surprise blackouts, dark window shades,
ration cards and Bundles for Britain.
Clean your plate: you know
the children in Europe are starving.

Sudden wail of sirens and arms pressing
head into school desk
as if a child's posture could keep me safe.
Air raids strafing perfect lawns
each proud to do its part.

When tickertape finally filled the sky
we strutted past bedtime,
ran pajama-clad into victory-swollen streets
banged pans and celebrated righteousness,

a palpitation alternated neurons
and the young blonde woman
back arched beneath that sailor's
Times square kiss,
never quite measured up in memory.

2

I missed Korea but went to Vietnam 1974,
and now I was in the field
though not a soldier
and not where patriotism wanted me.

Cuba to Paris, Paris to Moscow,
Moscow to Tashkent, Rangoon,
Vientane and onto Hanoi:
flowers of greeting
women wearing white headbands
of white hot grief.

It was six months before the end of a war
that devoured three million Vietnamese
and 58,000 Americans not counting
those who succumbed to Agent Orange
suicide and madness.

The war we lost, the one that left
a nation divided, raw,
the one our history books
call Vietnamese
and theirs American.

I had to show up to understand
Vietnam was a country,
not a war,
travel its narrow backbone
down Highway One
cross broad rivers where bridges

bombed for the twentieth time
became pontoon barges overnight
alive with people
who welcomed me with a smile,
flash of pain exploding in their eyes.

I went to meet an enemy
who was not my enemy,
listen to young peasant women
tell how they stretched their third-grade math
to bring the American bombers down.

Margaret Randall

How they entered tunnels where villagers
survived for years
cared for beloved water buffalo
even gave birth
and never doubted peace would come.

South of the 17th parallel
I bent to touch poisoned earth
where my government promised
nothing will grow for a thousand years,
learned courage would topple that promise.

3

Latin America's Dirty Wars caught me
on the ground in a decade
when orders were whispered
behind closed doors,
covert the name of every action.

We discovered the real meaning
of democracy then:
denial as code for
international treaties don't mean us,
torture a necessity and execution without trial
pride of The American Century.

I walked through battlefields
of Nicaraguan dead,
made the rounds to protect my neighborhood
through moist nights
watched my teenage daughters prepare for war.

I photographed the broken faces
of children in cheap coffins
wrote and published the news
my country kept from its headlines
made love and children and poems.

In Guatemala, Argentina and Uruguay
disappearance was the new weapon:
generations plucked one by one
from bedrooms and streets,
here one day, gone the next.

Those who survived might come home
with fangs implanted, mouths deformed
as message meant to warn anyone
daring take their place.

4

In the same backrooms, refurbished now,
over brandy or whiskey
or a line of coke
men reeking with power
catch sight of sun on desert walls,
lust for their Seven Cities of Gold.

War wins only itself, eternally,
while a president
who promises to stop the slaughter
wages another
then wins the big Peace Prize.

One day this language of lies
will fall on its own bayonet.
In Iraq, Afghanistan, Libya
or wherever the bully takes us next.

The Lie keeps shouting
have to finish what we started
right or wrong
while every drumbeat heartbeat life beat
pulses wrong and wrong.

Margaret Randall 55

Coda:

Have I forgotten the silenced wars,
Armenia's genocide
or Cambodia's Killing Fields,
once so urgent in the news?
Should I have said Rwanda?

Can I really salvage our gentle memories
set in the wrong direction,
bloodied, gutted,
tripping over themselves
as they drag us to this sad farewell?

Tenderness is not collateral damage,
partial lines scrawled across a page
found among the ruins
of all our lives.

Myra Shapiro

Lake Damariscotta

And the lake said, "I am a table."
And the trees said, "I'll surround you."
And the island said, "I'll be the centerpiece."
And I said, "I am here

May I sit?"
And I asked, "What will you serve?"

And the fish wouldn't answer
And the sun began to leave

But the waves took pity
And said *memory*.

Gold Star Girl

My job is to live. Like Isaac
named for laughter.
Not Job's job, up to his ears
in death. Tragedy

my mother knew when she lost
her first child; then I knew
she would die if I did—
so I didn't. My job is to live.

This year I'm seventy-five. *Good job*,
Mama'd say if she were here.
I hear it anyway. And soon
I will have to let her down.

Well, I must face it. Without
the comedy of an afterlife
there's only dying. How do I
find the mettle to give myself

to the violation? Run wild? Bear left?
You see what I'm up against.

The Bouquet

Nature frightened me—
you could die from it—
so I would stay in bed
with *A Child's Garden
of Verses*, rescued
from the heaving
and holding breaths
of asthma. Over
and over and
under my covers I read
"The Swing"—
that way I could fly
"up in the air so blue…"

Today wind enters my hair
as I walk in a field
of asphodel
and my heart skips
to William Carlos Williams,
his flower, his green
word, and I begin
to blabber sweetly to a bug,
"You are lovely
little crawling thing,
I wish I knew your name
so I could write a deeper poem."

My bug keeps crawling. Calling
it lovely gives me Galway,
his dreamy, milky sow, his blessing
to my mouth. Bless him
for remaining always near.

I wish Emily hadn't
just breezed by—
the buzz of that fly—
to cut me short.

Myra Shapiro 61

Stevenson must have known
up in the air so high
flies never stop on the sky.

March

Let me begin
though I am empty; I have nothing
to give. Let me
begin with nothing. The sperm
and the egg.
I am hungry. It is March,
the month
you always die, and suddenly
it's tomorrow.

The bus I'm traveling on jerks me up
and down.
A long wormy bus, two parts connected
in the center.
I sit in its middle, disconnected.
I don't want to
go where it's going. I don't want to stay
where it began.

I am begetting these words trying to get
out of the way
this day is turning. Without lunch.
Without keys.
Elsewhere is where
I must begin. On a bus. In words.

Death wants to let me in.
Tomorrow
I'll buy five purple iris to let you live, Mama,
as I have done
each March for thirty-three years.
March!

the month screams.
The bus is Limited.
I'll have to walk.
No lunch.

Myra Shapiro 63

At the End of the Play

Twice this month I've cried
at the end of a play, for the men
become disarmed and tender.

It's not Blanche made me weep
in *A Streetcar Named Desire,*
it's the gentleman caller she'd hoped for
sobbing against the wall.

"Make yourself an angel,"
the Victorian doctor's wife asks of him
in a new play. *In the Next Room.*

"Open your arms," and, like a child,
he does. In the snow he disrobes
for her. For all of us.
My husband and I hold his nakedness

close as we walk home—our 57th year
further in than we can climb out of.

"Let's have a brandy," he says.
"Yes, I'd like that," I answer.

Carole Stone

Inky Heart

I turn a corner,
see my parents down the
street,
    they who turn up
    everywhere.

I wave to them,
    as long-lost friends.

My lips form their names.
I say them as an invocation—
    Margaret, Harry—

they who live
as language
    in my inky heart.

Cigars

What this country needs is a good five cent cigar.
Thomas Riley Marshall

My father held a Corona Gigante
casually with three fingers.

My guardian uncle carried a short Churchill
in his mouth, wet, never lit.

Castro waved a Bolivar Fino like a flag,
bragging about power.

I loved to puff a cigarillo in the West Village
like "Vincent" Millay. Inhaling desire.

Rooftop

The mystery of blue
rooftop minarets, the Pacific beyond,
just as I imagined. In the distance,
two palms. Over my head, a flock

of gulls in formation flop
their way north, returning
to their first nesting place. How can I
reach my mother and father?

He's embalmed in whiskey. She's shrouded
in silver. They're not
in the sky, on land
or in the sea.

They row in me, jostling
my son, my daughter, my two granddaughters.
I won't let them
crowd my loves out.

Cross

God could have gotten Jesus down
from the Cross,

blood staining his side,
his gaunt body stretched out.

The same Old Testament deity
who didn't save the Jews

from going up in smoke.
It doesn't help

to be the Chosen people.
I look away

from such suffering, not believing
in Resurrection,

nor an eye for an eye,
a tooth for a tooth.

Yet hold absence in my heart,
like a small god.

Cold Edge

When the light—
if the light—
lifts me,
I will sniff a clam
alive in its shell,
touch a starfish

shining on the sand
like a diamond.
Nothing has changed

at the cold edge
of the Atlantic,
since I did

the dead man's float
as a girl.
When the dark—

if the dark—
brings back those who left,
I will sit on black rocks,

look at the hard stars,
the only person alive.
When the sea—

if the sea—
takes me to them,
as I tread far out,

almost mended,
I will ready myself
to go.

Florence Weinberger

Marrowbones

The fat women in the Coney Island steam bath
　　　　　pinched my cheek and laughed at nothing,
sweat gleaming off their skin and coarse, curly hair,
　　　　　not a bone to be seen anywhere,

not in my aunt's long breasts, none in the flesh
　　　　　of my mother's belly. I grew up in the shelter
of kitchen gossip, amplitude nourished by yeasty smells,
　　　　　pillows of soft, rising dough, a feminine language

that taught me where the body begins, its armature
　　　　　concealed, its health augmented like good soup.
By sixth grade, I knew I was fat. I married a man
　　　　　with a flat stomach and an unrequited hunger.

The soup the Nazis fed him in their concentration camp
　　　　　was thin as silk, what floated there thinner still.
From the aunts and mothers I learned wisdom is liquid,
　　　　　rescue, a recipe they give to their daughters.

When the soup is done, I remove the bones,
　　　　　scoop out the glutinous marrow, every last shred.
I spread it on fresh rye bread.
　　　　　I watch him eat, and my heart gets fat.

Florence Weinberger

Humming

I tend to hum in supermarkets. My daughter hears me two aisles away.
She asks me whether I know the market's song. She's being sarcastic.
I thought by now she'd outgrown her unwillingness to be seen with me.
But she makes me question what I'm doing. Am I praising or praying
earth's syncopation back to itself, scoping its music until the hum becomes
a hymn sung in layers like the ohms in the throats of Tibetan monks.

The other day I listened to a mass for four voices in a Gothic church.
Because they sang a cappella, I became the organ and the chimes,
I was the wooden pews worn to satin, I, the melancholy saints,
I, the flames, the shadows, I, the coins. I was the supplication.
Last night I heard a rabbi sing a word so softly it was sister to a hum
and the word *ru-achh* was the word for spirit and the word for wind.

To those who have brought my humming to my attention, who understand
that sometimes my hum is a whistle in the dark and sometimes it is grieving,
I give thanks. You have helped me know how one sound sets another
in motion, how thunder and gun shots are different tollings, and why this earth
is always shaking, though I must be honest, you haven't quite shown me
the source of that final quake, the one for which I seem to be rehearsing.

It's Not Chinatown

I'm on a bus in China, and it's raining, and I'm reading
O'Hara's poem, *The Day Lady Died*, for the second time
today, having bought a Dove bar at the last rest stop,
bypassing the fake Oreos and the dried black things
on the shelves. The familiar calls me home to New York
poetry. When will I know more than I know this time,
Lady's voice driven into my heart, on a gloomy Friday,
on the way to Shanghai, O'Hara on the way to
Easthampton, on a Friday. I feel our slightly parallel
journeys because I'm not at home just anywhere.
Who else on this bus would know who O'Hara's talking
about when he says Allen, Peter, Norman? There's
no news in China, only CNN headlines and baseball scores.
The picture-perfect canals in Suzhou hide the poor
behind their hung laundry. I had no heart to photograph
the girl going blind in the embroidery factory. Whoever
saw China in 2005 saw a thousand cranes, orange mantises
praying up skyscrapers. Men spitting on city sidewalks.
Smoke everywhere. *An Entire Country Killing Itself* blues.

Stephen Hawking's Reasoning

Though Hawking's body is a stem stuck in earth,
his mind stalks conjecture down fathomless holes.

And he figures out how something came from nothing.
Reports back through his computer *there is no god.*

In a universe that made him inert as a tree trunk,
spewing like a drunkard beyond its own boundaries,

havoc has no reason.

Surely Hawking's random genius grasps an irony
in which he praises nothing and is praised,

blames and thanks no one for a brain
that speeds as fast as light, and glows.

My two daughters drop me off at the museum

go for a walk if they were there I'd show them this painting
begun with a photograph a woman at her loom a woman
probably Chinese the artist's seal old-fashioned wooden
loom could be bamboo the woven cloth falling accrescent like
petals the painting teeming with allegorical birds do you think
what are you two talking about it's windy are they dressed
they are fine I am alone with their absence not every
eccentricity known to them when my mother died I thought
my father would burst into bloom but he died three months later
she is intact her stoic heart tucked inside beyond her lips
as drips and washes dissolve the photo the painting splits
she is a pillar still rooted fictional trees scatter their birds
leaflike the walls sprout flowers look. Look. Cross the street
carefully I love San Francisco you idiot they are grown women
they are married they have children their children grown I love
the way the painting derives a life from her interiority
am I the only one enthralled here while memory is passing
and the birds flock across the canvas escaping their
plumage pulsing a wing a feather a claw but you do get
it the mystery of her pulse complete I think that is what
they gave me 90 minutes we will meet back in the lobby
I should be done by then that is what they did in New York
would not come inside the Whitney to look at the Rothkos
I never taught them to look at a Rothko how could I when
scant time's left to browse from here there's more drift
what compels about this woman the concentration I think
it must be the incongruity or that is too glib you know
the creative *process* or day-dreaming or how she is going to
pay the rent no one standing next to me I am so lucky having
good weather and this is what I wanted to be celebrated on my
eightieth birthday with my two daughters no husbands no children
just us and I got to see this astonishing painting

Nellie Wong

When I am Breathing

> *I wanted to write you a letter*
> *But, my love, I don't know why it is,*
> *Why, why, why it is, my love,*
> *But you can't read*
> *And I—oh, the hopelessness—I can't write.*
>   Antonio Jacinto, "Letter from a Contract
>   Worker," *When My Brothers Come Home,*
>   *Poems from Central and Southern Africa*

When I am breathing, I am writing
I braid my daughter's hair
I lift my breast to my son's mouth

When I am writing, I am breathing
My sister and I herd sheep
On this vast land, the sky bluer
Than ink I am able to buy

My fingers pick each bean
From the pot of water
I hoist two buckets of water
Over my shoulders
And though they ache
I contemplate tomorrow
Not knowing if it will arrive

The song in my heart is a brook
Washing my body as I start the fire
Glancing at my daughter, my son
Crooning that their father will soon return

The rooster hops onto the bed
The orange cat nuzzles next to my youngest
Her eyes following the rattle I shake
I oil my son's scalp
and the writing flows from my fingertips

Wintry Interlude

Waiting in line at Wing Sing Bakery
as the rain falls over our heads,
my eyes roam
over the *cheern jook guern*, spring rolls
of *foo jook*, soybean skin, stuffed
with cellophane noodles and grass mushrooms,
the *gin duey*, voluptuous, deep-fried balls
of dough sprinkled with sesame seeds.
And there's the *joong*, known as
the Chinese tamale, stuffed
with sticky rice and boneless chicken.
My mouth waters as I wait patiently,
listening to the tall white guy
who says he works in construction
in Chinatown but buys his *dim sum*
here at three-tabled Wing Sing on Judah
while the Filipina in line nods as she names
all of *haw gow*, shrimp dumplings, chicken *siew mai*
and baked *cha siu bow* that she and her family
love when suddenly a young voice sings out,
"*Ng gaw bo low bao.*"
My attention turns to the young white man
with blue eyes and short-cropped hair
in the ubiquitous blue jeans and sweatshirt.
I say, "You speak Cantonese beautifully.
Where did you learn it?"
A smile blossomed as he answers,
"At Alice Fong Yu School."
"Was it required?" I continue.
"Yes, it's required."
He picks up the bagged order
of five pineapple buns,
putting three dollar bills onto the counter
as the woman clerk beams at him with
"*Dai yee wuey geen.*"
See you next time.
The boy bounces out of the store,
its window steamed, full of platters

of chicken on skewers, stuffed tofu,
don tot, egg tarts, *chow fun*, glistening rice noodles.

Consumed

Long Island, New York
Wal-Mart employee
39 years old, an African American man
A temporary worker
Stampeded to death at 5:00 A.M.
By 200 shoppers on Black
Friday, day after Thanksgiving
Who's to blame

Wal-Mart's lack of security?
Many waiting all night
For doors to open
At the crack of dawn?
Wal-Mart's statement
Through unseen suits
Sends their prayers
Who's to blame? The economic crisis?
People whose homes are being foreclosed?

People who don't know
If their next paycheck may be the last?
People in frenzy to buy
That flat-screen TV
That Nintendo game
That iPod, that Blackberry
That barbeque that will cook for hundreds
That Northface jacket
That rocking horse
That Armani knock-off
That pair of Nikes priced
At inflated dollars?

Who's to blame?
Who's to blame?
Who's to blame?

The Dow down 680 points
The official U.S. in recession
The terrorists in Mumbai
The stores opening up at 5:00 A.M.
Thanksgiving?

Woman In Red Shoes

She nods, her head sinks
Into her bosom
Toward her red shoes
Dreamland finds her
Holding an empty A&W root beer bottle,
Her fingers letting go and the bottle
Falls. Three times she lets go,
Three times a different passenger picks up
Her bottle, I'm the third, tucking it
Into her plastic sack with "Thank You" and a pink rose
Printed on it, holding a half-sandwich
Wrapped in waxed paper
Her red hat capes her black hair, she
A picture of serenity filling her gold jacket
With half moons, her black handbag hanging
Over the right arm of her wheelchair
Her skin the color of dark-roast coffee
Attracts the eyes of others, watching
The empty bottle fall, watching its return
To the woman in red shoes, asleep
For the twenty-minute ride
From San Francisco to West Oakland
When she suddenly awakens and wheels
Through the door onto the platform,
Her full body singing

I Know My Mother Better All the Time

I know my mother better all the time.
She leans on my shoulder, awake,
her hands dishing pancake flour
Can't follow her movements,
they are so quick, an eye-flash, in the kitchen.
Sugar, too, she scoops
with a Chinese soup spoon.

How to measure ingredients,
How to tell when the batter's just right
light as air, creamy and sensuous, soft as a woman's touch.
The heat becomes unbearable
and Ma's here.
Yes, she leans on me. No she climbs up on my shoulders,
her weight a gentle breeze,
she is quince blossoms on Chinese New Year's.
The oranges are tiny pyramids
topped with a tangerine
with a leaf symbolic of the family though we are spread
throughout California. We will gather to *hoy nien* to start
the New Year,
to forget work for one whole day.
Yes, Ma's here
telling us just how much soy sauce
to pour, how to crush the garlic
with the flat of the big knife.

I know my mother better all the time.
She lives inside me. Her hands and mine, our fingers,
knuckly twins. Together we shred
chicken for Chinese Chicken Salad,
we spread out on tables
winter melon soup, squab, duck
and the Monk's Dish
knowing that we feed ourselves
'cause Ma taught us
that self-sufficiency
means work

Nellie Wong 89

in the kitchen
and out on the streets.

Sondra Zeidenstein

In the Middle of the Night

Now that we've stopped "making love"
because my old bones hurt so
sometimes in the middle of the night
when you are asleep
and night lights make a path
for each of us through a different door
I wake heated by the moisture of our sleep
my nerves sparking with delight
and am joined to the memory of our loving
wherever our skins touch
my hand on your shoulder or back
or between your thighs
just below your sleeping sex I do not stir.

By day I'm often cranky, irritated:
the paces of our brains uneven
we fail to remember in the same way
the history we share. We are often
misaligned.
                    But now when you
are sound asleep in the heated bed
out the winter window not a single sound
in the house an occasional chewing in the walls
hot air knocking its way through base board pipes
I have you
                    an interlude I keep thinking
we'll look back on—too soon—
as a lull, a plateau before the steepest climbing.
You do not feel my touch
do not hear me whisper *my darling, my darling*
and *I love you so much*
love more insistent than clawing each other
in the greed of pleasure or the bliss of sleeping after sex
two as one.
                    I am all mouth, all skin
and yet there is no urgency, these nights
in our side by sideness, your body entrusted to mine
our breaths quiet, this reaching of my nerve endings

Sondra Zeidenstein 93

of my pores, all space between us closed.
I don't want to forget this in the days to come
of dying from each other. We have this.
I have it, this space sealed with tenderness.

Time Zones

When our daughter called us yesterday two hours later than her printed
itinerary said she'd be arriving on Air Emirates,

my husband George told her how worried he'd been, trying to figure out
what had gone wrong:

was her cell not working? had the plane taken off late? etc. He'd already tried
several times to call information,

to ask a synthetic voice for the phone number. He'd kept screaming at it:

emirates No, Em-ir-ates NO NO and slamming down the receiver.

When George's father was 85, a year more than George's age now,

he couldn't tolerate not being able to reach George by phone, getting our
answering machine

which gave no information about where we were and when we would be back

and when he finally reached us, he'd shout VER VASS YOU?

as if we'd done something terrible, as if he couldn't bear another disappear-
ance, another absence.

George's anxiety has increased over the years. And my annoyance at his anxiety.

All this by way of understanding our screaming fight in which I shouted: *I
don't want to be with you anymore*

and even *shut the fuck up*, usually a comic line of ours, and, seriously, *we're
going to have a terrible accident*

as we cooked five pots of cut up apples on the stove, their juices beginning to
sizzle,

Sondra Zeidenstein 95

so hot their sugar would burn our skin off if we'd spilled some on us. We who rarely fight,

in our dotage, our gentle voices genuine, we know we'll lose one another, sooner than later.

Of course we calmed down, worked the huge, soft batches of hot apples through *mr squeezo,*

cranking it, collecting out of its spout into big bowls, apple sauce, twenty-three containers in all for the coming winter.

Then we relaxed over spaghetti, a bit of leftover salad, an evening of television. In the same time zone.

Rarely in the same time zone.

At age fourteen George's father had swum across a river out of Russia with guns firing at him,

leaving behind his mother and baby sister he'd never see again.

George, as a boy, had watched over his epileptic mother who'd have seizures in department stores

in which he'd lose sight of her, then find a crowd gathered around her unconscious and usually rigid body,

move the crowd back and take charge, *this is my mother.*

Can you follow this? I have to,

as I had to live, in the early years of our marriage, in fear of an edginess like my father's from an even earlier time zone, until I learned to yell back

any time George lost his temper, no longer afraid I'd be left alone if I did.

Getting happier and happier, we've made it through our long marriage,

clinging to each other now, loving the curve of his palm on my wrist,

the pressure of the present on each other, our bodies' adjustments

until we go to sleep, very close, and when we wake to pee I apologize

for losing my temper and he apologizes for losing his and we lie down again,

in the same time zone, to sleep a few more hours.

Subjection of Women

It is all there in the Romanian movie: *Four Months, Three Weeks, Two Days*:

slim white legs the pregnant student waxes before going to the abortionist,

the girlfriend who goes with her, loyal, protective of her helpless friend

who is not smart or wary, just looking for the cheapest fix

and doesn't anticipate the price for ending a five month pregnancy,

the hotel guarded at the desk by indifferent clerks asking for money, ID, papers,

room like a cell,

slim innocent body the coarse, beaten down abortionist rapes.

He rapes the girlfriend too. After all, he is risking ten years in jail.

The abortionist provides an alcohol wash of the genital area and a long narrow
tube called a probe in the translation from Romanian

that he sticks into her slowly—camera is on the innocent, narrow knees—until
it stings

which means it's poking into her womb, her uterus

and tells her to lie absolutely still until she feels she has to go to the bathroom

and "let it all come out":

in the movie a doll obviously, rouge smeared, but gruesome in a bunch of towels
on the bathroom floor.

The loyal girlfriend takes it under her coat, out into the middle of the night,

no electricity at that hour, roving, half starved dogs, merciless garbage chutes
on the roof.

What else can you do, who else do you have to help you in this place?

She dumps the doll baby down a chute with a few silent prayers.

This is what it means to be a woman.

Like the old woman my friend knows, who was trapped in her laundry room for hours,

too dry for the rapist to get into,

promising him money, anything if he will just let her go.

She wouldn't go out for a year afterwards.

Above all, don't move, the abortionist said, and left her waiting.

Alan Ginsburg
(after reading his collected letters)

A week bad bursitis, couldn't walk, sit long, can't swim as planned.

Read day long, middle of night, finished 500 pages almost Alan Ginsburg
letters, fifty years worth.

Love this man. Didn't believe in holding back. In his letters, too, says every-
thing.

Almost contemporaries. I came N.Y. 1953, just married, pregnant,

he at Columbia writing poetry, at first formal lines, cryptic meaning
like most 50's poets I read, couldn't understand,

young mother, Harvard MA, pretty baby daughter, fading onto the park
bench by the sand box, staring at color of sand.

Then found his voice. Kerouac stream of words influenced him, reporting
movement of mind, line based on breath, line almost poem in itself,

didn't censor, or not much, compressed but still intelligible,

loved Blakean vision, spent years traveling on drugs, always young lovers,
queer poet, multiple lovers in same bed,

need to be loved, touched, need for *love come release,*

loved naked, sometimes naked on stage, loved making private public, raw
consciousness uncensored, gets you to truth, what's real, wild rush, gushers of
vision

in a hurry to tell all, even embarrass self he sd reading out poem about mas-
turbating with broom stick in hotel bathroom, but proud to liberate univer-
sal shame around that.

Later Buddhist influence.

He took on everyone, know it all. His letters scolded academy, academics, those who suppressed me, made me fussy, harsh teacher at first, only one culture allowed, one grammar, one syntax.

Come to last letters, diagnosis liver cancer a few days left,

asks Clinton to give him national poet honor, means it, I think,

but understand not possible, he says, if trouble for Clinton with Gingrich.

Finished book, miss him today.

Gives so much in these letters, I look into skull, heart, cock, asshole for love outrage.

Do not censor this man. Do not censor me, changed, when Alan changed poetry landscape,

from self regarding timid girl woman, careful hairdo, eyebrows, lipstick, hose, seams, heels, everything kept in, kept down, thin poet longing for nakedness,

wild never my nature, but love Alan, understand desire to disrobe for maximum power.

Don't be cautious. Then what can harm me?

Sondra Zeidenstein 101

History

I was twenty-five, in Brooklyn, with two toddlers,
when I watched nine black children in their Sunday best
stopped by the Little Rock National Guard,
bayonets drawn, white women hooting,
their faces twisted with hatred, at least one of them
spitting on the girl whose skirt was prettily puffed by petticoats.

Fifty years later, here I am, my eyes fixed on Gwen Ifill
near fifty, on a segment of the News Hour
with the Little Rock Nine. Fiftieth anniversary—
1957, ancient history—of their having "integrated"
the high school in Little Rock which had never had
a black student in its halls. Gwen asks them, her elders,

in a reverent voice, her face without the usual television makeup,
no polish to her cheeks, her hair worn old-fashioned southern,
asks them how they are feeling *today.*
"I knew that woman, the one who spit on me.
I remember the shock," she says, "the whole year like that."
There will be blood in the streets—we see the clip,

Governor Faubus of Arkansas–*if these children try to enter.*
We see Eisenhower's bald head lean toward the camera,
signing the children a federal escort. "When I left school each day
I didn't know where I'd get the courage to go back."
We, the remnant of those who watched, remember
the hollow of the mouth that spit. "It's so hard

to come together this way, it brings back the *emotions,*"
she said, the little girl, her brightly polished shoes,
tight belt, books under her arm, the little girl
who had the strength to get up each morning
to be humiliated, scared—doing this, how could she know?
for Gwen someday, who would do it someday for the Rutgers Five,

doing it even for me sitting against an icepack pressed
to my upper spine for nerve pain that's keeping me down these days,
restoring me, in whose old brain *1957* is inscribed, *to hope.*

Geraldine Zetzel

Worldly Goods

Those teachings about *Impermanence*
—I know, I know—yes, but what to do
            —right now, I mean—
with this flood of leftovers
—these lifetimes muttering
            in every cupboard?

This set of open-work ivory linen
            we bought in Florence—place mats
            runner, a dozen napkins to match
My parent's wedding silver—complete with
            twelve oyster forks, ten butter-knives
            & six egg-spoons washed in gold

And here are the cigarette boxes & ashtrays
                  we used to put out for parties
here the leaky beautiful Raku vessels
from my days as a potter

Nobody wants our Danish Blue wedding china
or the treasured record collection—
            Casals playing Bach Suites, Burl Ives,
            Dylan Thomas—(oh that bardic, drunken voice)
            The Play of Daniel, Guys and Dolls, Candide…

And what to do with videos of birthdays & graduations
            boxes full of photo negatives—carefully catalogued?
These journals of trips—each day recorded
            with notes, addresses of people we met
receipts from famous restaurants—
The Dordogne—Sicily—The Fjords of Norway.
Guidebooks—Indonesia & Mexico & Greece?
            And maps, oh those marked & re-folded maps…
His pocket Atlas—
our cancelled passports

And then there's this mountain of books
            Who now will want

Geraldine Zetzel

Masefield's Collected Works bound in leather?
The Oxford Companion to English Literature (1948)?
& all the slim volumes of essays & poetry,
        fly-leaves inscribed with the names
        of old lovers & dead friends…

Ah tell me anyone—how do I travel light,
all these beloved useless things
clinging to my legs like so many children
        babbling their stories?
Are they afraid of the dark?
What shall I tell them…
        how can I comfort them?

Lying

Sometimes a lie is a lioness
kept in a private menagerie
by a man in Ohio. One October night
he decides—who knows why
—to let all his animals go.
One paw at a time, the big cat
leaves the familiar cage,
goes forth to explore the town.
Into a world of backyard grills
and garbage cans,
and the heady smells
of barbecue and apples.

I used to keep lies like that
for the joy of lying, for the power.
I loved them, kept them well-hidden,
taught them tricks. Big lies
that would come to me when called.
Little ones that knew how to *Roll Over*,
Play Dead, innocent as puppies.

❀   ❀   ❀

A child sits in front of her dinner
and will not be excused until
she's chewed and swallowed
everything on her plate.
Grownups have left the table, gone
to chat and smoke in the living-room
over black coffee and cigarettes.

If you don't eat, she's told,
you're going to be sent away
to a place where children like you
are fattened like geese—
if they refuse to eat, the nurses
use a tube and a funnel…

Geraldine Zetzel   109

That's what they said: I knew
it was a lie, but that lie had legs.
So I chewed on and on for years,
secretly fed my own lies
the scraps and gristle
under the table.

❀　❀　❀

And my own children?
I gave them the truth, as I knew it
—they were free to eat it or not,
put ketchup on it or not
leave on their plates or
feed it to the dog.

And one day I let my own lies
go free. I don't miss them.
Sometimes they leave
muddy tracks on the porch.
Once in a while I set out
a dish of milk for them.
Or a lump of salt.

Carmelina
after Matisse

You sit facing us
mantled in sunlight,
sturdy and whole
as a loaf of new bread.
Shadows define
your body.
At your belly's center
the deep well of the navel
is a promise of plenty.

Like a beacon you glow against
the ochre of the wall,
the gray of an empty fireplace.
The artist is a red blotch
in the mirror,
trying to set down
on canvas this unabashed wonder—
no more wonderful to him, perhaps,
than the blue jug on the table,
no more sexual
than a bunch of tulips.

What is there to stare at?
remarks your gaze.
No odalisque or nymph,
you wear your nakedness
like a robe of clear water.

(If one dared touch that skin
or the heavy braid of hair
it would be like touching
the flank of a lioness.)

How do I learn this ease?
To drop the self—its shame,
its complicated appetites
and its lies,

Geraldine Zetzel 111

as casually as you've dropped
that pink towel
across one thigh?

Joy

A wet leaf glints in the sun
a jay calls out in the woods

Coolness touches my face
for a moment: this edge of joy

how it comes and goes, teasing
like the edge of foam that rides

the beach ahead of each wave
to be swallowed with a sigh

into wet sand until the next one
rises, and the next

Mt. Fuji Between the Waves
Off the Coast of Kanagawa

That morning, Master, we hastened to the beach at dawn. It was very
 cold. In winter, there is much sickness, so only a few of us are able to
 go forth. Just three boats went out that day. Hunger, however, knows
 nothing of these matters and the fish do not take note of the
 fishermen. The air was so cold it cut like ice in the wash-bucket.
 Each man who owned a quilted coat made haste to put it on.

Beyond the Holy Mountain the sky was dark grey; over the sea
 it was pale as cold ashes. The sea itself was ink, black and
 ready and silent.

We launched our longboats, eight men at oars and the captain on the
 foredeck. For six hours we cast our nets. Never in all my days—
 and I am the oldest man in our village—have I seen such a run of
 fish! Then the wind began to blow from the North; the sea began
 to speak. Captains shouted back and forth between the boats,
 Should we turn back? Shall we go on? They could not agree.

The Holy Mountain watches us, lifting her white brow above a cloak
 of blue. One boat turns back and makes for shore. Waves cover it
 from sight; we do not see it again. The sky is a shining
 mirror, the wind speaks in a hundred tongues. Great claws of foam
 reach out from the peak of each wave. Our boats carve through the
 enormous swells. Leaning over the oars, we labor like ants that
 try to move a leaf through tall grass, We groan like women in child-
 birth. The steersmen cry out as each wave approaches. Their cries are
 lost in the howl of the seas.

A giant wave appears from the West. It reaches for us with a
 thousand arms, a thousand hands, a thousand mouths. The sea
 roars with hunger. Gobbets of foam as big as summer hailstones
 pelt down on our backs. Our lungs are breaking. The nets wash
 overboard.

Only for a moment do I stop to wipe the foam and salt from my eyes.
In the distance, beneath a sky patterned rose and pale-grey
like the kimono of a maiden, I behold Mt. Fuji, small as the
little hill where the children go for firewood.

Master Hokusai, this is all I remember.

About the Poets

Betty Buchsbaum

I wrote poetry often as a young girl, but the impulse went underground for years. As a professor I often wrote about, and taught, other poets. However, with the birth of a granddaughter when I was in my forties, the desire to write, pretty constantly, surfaced; and to write about intimate feelings and relationships. Here poets like Sharon Olds and Adrienne Rich emboldened me. Now, in my eighties, I seem to write primarily as a witness to my own aging—its adjustments, losses, difficult times and, yes, simple pleasures, joys and yearnings. My publications include a book-length collection, *The Love Word* (Chicory Blue Press, 2004) and various journals and anthologies including *Prairie Schooner, Women's Review of Books, Salamander, Solo, Lilith, Spoon River Review, Kalliope, Family Reunion, Her Face in the Mirror*. I have given readings in libraries, bookstores and colleges in New England and New York. Two of my poems have won prizes.

Phoebe Hoss

I have been writing poetry all my life – probably for seventy-five of my eighty-seven years. I have written it through, and about, good times and bad. Until relatively late in life, I wrote largely for myself and thought of myself in terms of my two major preoccupations: mother of two and editor of scholarly books. When I retired in 1992, however, I set to work on a memoir and began to take part in poetry workshops. Now I consider myself a poet, though I'm happy still to be a mother and, now, a grandmother. I haven't published widely. One poem was published in *Barrow Street*, and others have appeared in various nonprofit books: *Five Hundred Tuesdays* by the Wellfleet Writers Guild; *World of Water, World of Sand: A Cape Cod Collection of Poetry, Fiction and Memoir; River Voices* by the Poets of Stuyvesant Cove Park in New York City; and *Offerings II*, poems by members of the Unitarian Church of All Souls, also of New York City (I edited the last two of these publications). In 2012, I self-published *A Stairway Unfurling: A Lifetime of Poems*. Since I am still writing and have a backlog of poems, I am thinking of bringing out another volume next year.

Nancy Kassell

As a girl and young woman, I wrote very few poems, but I read fervently. It seemed obvious then that to be a poet, you had to be male. As a classical scholar, I taught Greek and Roman poets, and published articles on Horace and Ovid in academic journals. I also published a book, a feminist cultural study of the

Greco-Roman legacy in America, and essays in the *New York Times*. Finally, twenty years ago when I was in my mid-fifties, I began to write my poetry and discovered a medium that admitted many selves. Two poets I especially admire are Marie Ponsot, with whom I studied at the Fine Arts Work Center in Provincetown, MA, and Wislawa Szymborska. My work has appeared in *Notre Dame Review, BORDERLANDS, Eclipse, Willow Springs, Peregrine, Salamander,* and *Spoon River Poetry Review*, as well as in the anthologies *Verse and Universe: Poems about Science and Mathematics,* and *Family Reunion: Poems about Parenting Grown Children*. My translation of Zuzanna Ginszanka, "Non omnis moriar" from the Polish (with Anita Safran), the first English translation of this poem, appeared on *AgniOnline*. I have given readings in the Boston area and in New York City. My first book of poetry, *Text(isles)*, is forthcoming from Dos Madres Press.

Rita Brady Kiefer

Writing—for me—is like feeling a constant friend from the other side helping me understand—gradually—what it means to be human. It mines my unconscious and reveals to me the mystery that is Rita, joining me to other humans in the deepest way. It is more permanent than contemplation, more personal than prayer. I have loved this act since I was six, abandoned it in my late teens then returned to it with passion in my early forties. Emily Dickinson was right: *publication IS the auction of the mind,* but I have sought to have my work read. Fortunately two chapbooks, *Unveiling* (Chicory Blue Press) and *Trying on Faces* (Monkshood Press) as well as a full-length collection, *Nesting Doll* (University Press of Colorado) have been published. "My Name Is Not Eve," my play that explores the stories of four survivors of domestic violence, was performed in Denver and other Colorado venues. For the past 25 years I have facilitated weekly writing sessions in women's shelters. Still it is the act of putting words on paper that makes me able to live as a seeker in this beautiful/terrifying world, and in the end it is writing that sustains me.

Liane Ellison Norman

A writer all my life, I rediscovered poetry in my old age. My most recent book of poems, *Breathing the West: Great Basin Poems,* was published by Bottom Dog Press in the fall of 2012, the same year in which a chapbook, *Driving Near the Old Federal Arsenal,* was released by Finishing Line Press. I published individual poems in the *North American Review, Kestrel, The Fourth River, 5 AM, Grasslimb,*

Rune, Hot Metal Press and in *Voices From the Attic* and *Come Together: Imagine Peace* anthologies. I won the Wisteria Prize for poetry in 2006 from Paper Journey Press and have published two earlier books of poetry, *The Duration of Grief* and *Keep*. I have also published a book about nonviolent protest against nuclear bomb parts makers, *Mere Citizens: United, Civil and Disobedient*; a biography, *Hammer of Justice: Molly Rush and the Plowshares Eight*; a novel, *Stitches in Air: A Novel About Mozart's Mother* and many articles, essays and reviews.

Margaret Randall

I have been writing ever since I was six and learned how. As a very young woman, I knew writing would be central to my life. I think of myself primarily as a poet, but among my more than 100 published books there are also many of oral history and essay. I also often use my photography in conjunction with the written word. I was born in 1936, so came of age in a country besieged by McCarthyism and the chill it placed on creative expression. Fortunately, I moved to Latin America in 1961, where I co-founded and edited a bilingual literary journal out of Mexico City for the following eight years. Contact with poets south of the border and around the world, helped me extradite myself from the McCarthyist idea that made political poetry taboo. In fact I do not believe there are political poems, only successful and unsuccessful ones. A poem can be about anything if it is well made, if it take risks and surprises. Now, as I age, I am freer to devote more time to my writing. I have a very supportive partner, also an artist, and our relationship is centered on her painting and my writing. I believe in the power of language to effect change in the world. My most recent books of poetry are *Stones Witness* (University of Arizona Press, 2007), *Ruins* (University of New Mexico Press, 2011), *Something's Wrong With the Cornfields* (Skylight Press, 2011), *Where Do We Go from Here?* (Wings Press, 2012), and *The Rhizome as a Field of Broken Bones* (Wings Press, 2013). Coming in September, also from Wings Press, will be *Daughter of Lady Jaguar Shark*.

Myra Shapiro

As a sickly child I found order and comfort in poems. As a mother and high school English teacher in Tennessee, I had the chance to bring that deep pleasure toward my life with others. The year my mother died, in my mid-forties, I began steadily to write poems. I sublet an apartment in NYC to study and work in a community of poets. My 50th birthday I celebrated with a U.C. Berkeley trip to Greece and Sicily with Robert Bly followed by a summer workshop with

Galway Kinnell and Sharon Olds. Not long after, Poets House was born and I was asked to serve on its board. My poems began being published in periodicals and anthologies, and in 1996 my first book, *I'll See You Thursday. 12 Floors Above the Earth* was published in 2012, and a memoir *Four Sublets: Becoming a Poet in New York* in 2007. In 1999 and 2003 my poems were included in *The Best American Poetry.*

Carole Stone

After reading the poetry of Paul Lawrence Dunbar, at twelve I wrote my first poem about "a little 'ole tomcat jumpin' on a mouse." From the beginning I wrote of oppression, partly because of persecution in the world at large, and partly because of my identification with minorities arising out of being brought up by an aunt after my parents' early death when I was four. My lost mother and father have functioned as my muse throughout my lifetime, as I have imagined and re-imagined them in my travels to England, Ireland, Russia, and other countries and associated them with literary figures like Isaac Babel and movie stars like Carole Lombard. Present family has been a vital source for my poems as I have gone on to write about my son and daughter, two granddaughters and my brother, witness to our childhood. Cultural figures and history are a source of creativity as well: Josephine Baker, George Gershwin, and Prohibition and poets from the Harlem Renaissance writers to Marina Tsetayeva, Paul Celan and Anna Akhmatova, among others. Writing poetry has sustained me intellectually and emotionally as a source of pleasure from language and the intellectual process of revision, as a way of recovering and recreating my parents, and now, grown older, aging. With poetry I found a community for the family I lost. I have published seven chapbooks of poetry and three full-length books. The two most recent books are *American Rhapsody*, CavanKerry Press, 2012 and *Hurt, The Shadow The Josephine Hopper Poems*, Dos Madres Press, 2013.

Florence Weinberger

The physical act of writing took hold of me in first grade, with my earnest efforts to perfect my handwriting. By fourth grade I was writing the class Halloween play, and at the age of 13, I was accused of plagiarism. It never occurred to me to say *I am a writer* anymore than having to announce *I am a girl*, until the 60's, when I AM WOMAN became a political statement. Yet it took me years to say, when asked what I do, *I am a poet.* I have published four books of poetry, *The Invisible Telling Its Shape*, Fithian Press, 1997, *Breathing Like a Jew*, Chicory Blue

Press, 1997, *Carnal Fragrance*, Red Hen Press, 2004, and *Sacred Graffiti*, Tebot Bach, 2010. Among my awards are first prizes in the Poetry/LA Bicentennial, Sculpture Gardens Review, Mississipi Valley, Red Dancefloor and the dACenter for the Arts poetry contests.

Nellie Wong

I have published three books of poetry plus a chapbook during the 40-plus years when my first collection, *Dreams in Harrison Railroad Park*, was released in 1977, the most-published book in Kelsey Street Press's history (four printings). My following books are *The Death of Long Steam Lady* (Westside Press, 1986), *Stolen Moments* (Chicory Blue Press, 1997) and *Breakfast Lunch Dinner* (Meridien PressWorks, 2012). My poems and essays have appeared in numerous anthologies, journals and other publications. I was co-featured in the documentary film, "Mitsuye and Nellie Asian American Poets," by Allie Light and Irving Saraf. In 2011, I was honored by having a building named after me at my alma mater, Oakland High School, Oakland, CA. Two of my poems are engraved on public sites in San Francisco as part of the San Francisco Municipal Railway projects. Retired as a Senior Analyst in Affirmative Action, I continue to write and journey into the night.

Sondra Zeidenstein

I grew up on poetry. From the age of three, I read anthologies of poems until their covers fell off and their pages bloated and frayed. But I wrote nothing of my own. Fiercely withdrawn, I couldn't even imagine that possibility. I just read and studied and taught. I started writing at the age of fifty, as the result of therapy; I burst open after a half century of repression, and have never stopped. My early teachers and guides, models of women's daring, were Honor Moore and Joan Larkin. I have been a follower of Sharon Olds since she began publishing and have attended many week-long workshops, where she wrote with us, at Squaw Valley and Omega and on white water canoe retreats led by wilderness guide Beverly Antaeus. I continued my education as a poet in poetry critiquing groups and with peer poets from whom I drew the courage to continue my sort of writing. My poems have been published in journals and anthologies. My poetry collections include *A Detail in that Story* and, most recently, *Contraries*. I am editor of *Family Reunion: Poems about Parenting Grown Children* and *A Wider Giving: Women Writing after a Long Silence*. I am publisher of Chicory Blue Press, focusing on the writing of older women.

Geraldine Zetzel

Growing up tri-lingual made me deeply aware of language from early on. I began writing poetry early—I still have a sonnet I wrote in 5th grade—and continued on and off into early adulthood. Several fallow periods later, I began to write again, using poetry as a means of understanding my world, both exterior and interior, more deeply. In old age, partly by being a member of a very insightful and supportive group of fellow-poets, I find myself more and more committed to my own writing. And more open, too, to the pleasures of reading the work of other poets. Among other influences, the poets I tend to turn to again and again include Elizabeth Bishop, Jane Hirshfield, Stanley Kunitz, Lisel Mueller, Sharon Olds, and Tomas Tranströmer. My most recent publication is a full-length collection, *Mapping the Sands* (Mayapple Press, 2010). I am the author of two chapbooks, *Near Enough to Hear the Words* (Pudding House Publications) and *With Both Hands* (Finishing Line Press). A group of poems and an interview were featured in the anthology, *A Wider Giving* (Chicory Blue Press). Other poems have appeared in a number of anthologies and journals.

Credits

Phoebe Hoss: "Oh Carapace!" "A Splotch of Yellow" "Ms Maybe Resists the Sirens' Song" "Message to Hamas" from *A Stairway Unfurling: A Lifetime of Poems* by Phoebe Hoss, 2012.

Rita Brady Kiefer: "Meteors" first appeared in *Malala: Poems for Malala Yousafzai*, ed. Joseph Hutchison and Andrea L. Watson (FutureCycle Press, 2013).

Liane Ellison Norman: "Knitting Needle" "Rules" "Inheritance" "Flick of a Bird" from *Breathing the West: Great Basin Poems*, Bottom Dog Press, 2012.

Margaret Randall: "Wherever You Are, Lois Lane" from *Something's Wrong with the Cornfields*, Skylight Press, London and Boulder, 2011, "Every Equation Up For Grabs" "Writing on the Body" "Wrong and Wrong" and "Clean Red and Black" from *The Rhizome as a Field of Broken Bones*, Wings Press, San Antonio, Texas, 2013.

Myra Shapiro: "Gold Star Girl" from *12 Floors Above the Earth* by Myra Shapiro, Antrim House, 2012.

Carole Stone: "Inky Heart" "Cigars" "Rooftop" from *American Rhapsody* by Carole Stone, CavanKerry Press, 2012.

Florence Weinburger: "Marrowbones" "Humming" "It's Not Chinatown" from *Sacred Graffiti* by Florence Weinberger, Tebot Bach, 2010. "Stephen Hawking's Reasoning" was published in *Solo Nuevo*. "My two daughters drop me off at the museum" was published, with Honorable Mention, in *Passager*.

Nellie Wong: "I Know My Mother Better All the Time" from *Breakfast Lunch and Dinner* by Nellie Wong, Meridien Press Works, 2012. "Consumed" was first published in outlawpoetry.com 2010/07/01. "Wintry Interlude" was first published (online) in *Big Bridge Anthology of Bay Area Women Writers*, ed by Katherine Hastings, 2000.

Sondra Zeidenstein: "Subjection of Women" "Allan Ginsburg" "History" from *Contraries* by Sondra Zeidenstein, Chicory Blue Press, 2011.

Geraldine Zetzel: "Carmelina" "Joy" "Mt. Fuji Between the Waves off the Coast of Kanagawa" from *Mapping the Sands* by Geraldine Zetzel, Mayapple Press, 2010.

Order Form

Chicory Blue Press, Inc.
795 East Street North
Goshen, CT 06756
(860) 491-2271
(860) 491-8619 (fax)
sondraz@optonline.net
www.chicorybluepress.com

Please send me the following books:

_____ copies of *Speaking for my Self: Twelve women poets in their seventies and eighties* edited by Sondra Zeidenstein at $18.00

_____ copies of *Contraries: New and Selected Poems* by Sondra Zeidenstein at $18.00

_____ copies of *Four Sublets: Becoming a Poet in New York* by Myra Shapiro at $18.00

_____ copies of *What if your mother* by Judith Arcana at $15.00

_____ copies of *Resistance* by Sondra Zeidenstein at $18.00

_____ copies of *The Love Word* by Betty Buchsbaum at $18.00

_____ copies of *Family Reunion: Poems about Parenting Grown Children*, edited by Sondra Zeidenstein at $18.00

Name _____

Address _____

_____

Connecticut residents: Please add sales tax.

Shipping: Add $4.00 for the first book and $1.50 for each additional book.